D1431943

Overcoming My Personal Demons

One mans contribution for a better world

Timothy Spigelmeyer jr

Spigelmeyer jr

DEDICATION

This book is dedicated to my children. You may not have always understood my motivations, but I promise you they were bigger than you ever imagined. I love all of you.

CONTENTS

Spigelmeyer jr

ACKNOWLEDGMENTS

I have many to thank for the writing of this book but first and foremost I thank GOD for providing me with the strength to face my fears and overcome my personal demons through experiences that have allowed me to learn and grow into my true essence.

Thank you to my family, friends and children who have supported me throughout all my missteps.

Thank you, Jan Marie, for being the guiding light in my life right when I needed it most.

To my grandmother Elsie, I miss you every single day. Thank you for all you have done for me.

Thank you all, I love you deeply
more than you will ever know.......

1. The Beginning

"THE BEGINNING IS THE MOST IMPORTANT PART
OF THE WORK." ~ PLATO

The story of me began on Saturday July 1st, 1978 in Lancaster County, Pennsylvania. I was born at the Lancaster General Hospital to my parents who had divorced when I was young so I will only give accounts of my life from the moments that I remember. My memory begins in Elizabethtown, a small town rooted in the heart of Lancaster County, which at the time didn't appear to have many worldly worries upon it, or so it seemed to me, then again we all have skewed pictures in our minds when we are young about just what it is we are up against. This area had and still does have a large Amish and Quaker influence whose communities provided most of the farming and crop distribution to much of the state. I was raised by my father and stepmother each of whom brought with them a daughter as well, three girls and two boys, we were outnumbered for sure. My father and I

1

never really had much of a relationship, which I still think about today, mostly because I have children of my own that I have failed to maintain a closeness with, but like they say, recognition is the first step in change and I have certainly recognized a lot about myself through the process of transformation. I never really got to know my father on a deep level until later in life, but I know he was just doing the best he could with what he knew. I may, at the time, have had a grudge for his lack of compassion towards us but I have come to love deeply these days, and I see him through a different set of eyes. Him and my biological mother separated when I was young and I only really saw her in tiny bits growing up, typically certain weekends here and there, but those moments I did get in her presence will come to have an impact on my choices later in life. We would have nice times together, but she was in a different state of mind back in those days. Her and her new husband at the time were more into a partying lifestyle drinking or smoking marijuana quite regularly which must have implanted something into my subconscious mind as you will come to learn. We had some nice times together, but we didn't really grow any sort of deep relationship, looking back I feel she was just going through the motions of her responsibility to us. She would take us to visit with our grandparents on occasion but not often enough to even get to know them. I remember my grandfather being a guitar player, a marathon runner, a lover of woodworking and an Army veteran but that was about it. Even though I didn't know him on a personal level, he will come to have a profound influence on me and my journey as well. My stepmother was and still is a great woman in my eyes, we weren't deeply close but she cared about us, she cared enough to be the enforcer of the rules, to hold us accountable for our actions and instill in us a discipline I would later come to absolutely love her for. She was the type of mother who set rules for us, we were made to clean our bedroom certain days of the week, she would inspect them and ensure we did it properly, there wasn't any dust where we were to be dusting and what she laid out for us to do, we did or we got punished, there wasn't a shortage of punishment in my household growing up I assure you of that. Both my sisters were older than me but the three of us got along and had good times together playing and sharing in the normal childhood activities of our time. Each of us played sports in some capacity and enjoyed playing outside as much as we could. I'll never forget the time the three of us were playing outside one night after it had snowed a pretty heavy snow, the planet at that time was still cool enough that I remember when the snow came deep and heavy almost every year. We used to have an old tire swing in our backyard that was tied to a high tree branch with three separate pieces of rope in one, it was always a thing for me to stand on the top of the tire and pull the rope apart like a bow and arrow, standing in between the pieces while the tire would swing. We all three were loaded up with snow gear that night and I remember we were outside throwing snowballs at each other. I decided that I would be the funny guy and stand on the tire, in between the ropes, mind you it is cold outside, the tire is wet from the snow, turning this into a slick situation. I remember getting on top of the tire, pulling the ropes apart and getting nailed with a snowball right in the head. I immediately lost my grip, fell backwards losing my hold on the ropes allowing them to close tightly around my ankle. I was dangling upside down like a rabbit caught in a snare screaming for them to help get me down, which they did, but not until they laughed at me for a little while leaving me to swing in the cold. We had good times together as a family, we enjoyed family activities like camping or attending the local zoos and fairs. We weren't a wealthy family, we didn't do or have a ton of lavish things, we were a simple working-class family, like so many others, just trying to get by in those days. Our family did not have a religious focus either, we did not attend church regularly or even pray before meals nor did we even really talk about GOD. My fathers' mother, my grandmother was the only one I remember who talked about religion, the only one who owned a bible back then and she was the only one who tried pushing us all in that direction. Although I didn't listen to her, she will end up becoming one of the biggest saviors to me in this story as well as best friend in life.

I attended the Elizabethtown Area School district for most of my schooling years, except I believe my first year in elementary which was at school located just outside of town. Academia was not for me, I did not like school as far back as I could remember, for whatever reason at the time school caused a ton of friction in my life. Now that I am older and a lot wiser, I certainly appreciate every chance to learn and expand my mind. I remember I was always the attention getter in class, the class clown as some like to call it, maybe it was a lack of attention at home or a feeling of not having cohesion that made me act out. I was disruptive and always looking to be the center of attention even when the teacher was speaking. I will not use names in these stories because it is not my intention to bring any negative light to anyone, just shed light on my behavior, my actions and how I have come to be. I remember one incident early on in grade school where a teacher tied me to my chair with a jump rope because of how disruptive I was being in class. Yes, you read that correctly, I got tied to my chair with a jump rope because of my behavior. Stay with me folks this only gets better as the years go on, I promise. When I really applied myself to the class work and the materials, I would do great with it, I could excel and get good grades but something within me just did not want to do that, something in me was telling me grades didn't matter, school work didn't matter, what mattered more to me was the interactions with everyone. I cared and got along with everybody, I wasn't bullied, I wasn't a bully myself, I genuinely could have a relationship with all my classmates and even my teachers to a certain degree. When I think about my past actions today from the view of my current state of spirituality it all makes sense to me. The future certainly does prove the past as you will come to find out.

At a fairly young age I can recall being attracted to the arts, whether it was music, conventional art such as painting or drawing or singing, the ability to create from my imagination was immensely strong throughout the entirety of my life. I remember the praises I would get from teachers as well as family and friends about my natural creative abilities. I had and still do have a huge imagination, I always loved to dream big, dream about fantastical things and try creating them in some shape or form through my natural talents. I had an immense passion for the outdoors as well, at that age I wanted to be outside all the time, whether I was riding bike, playing monster trucks in the yard, or playing in the woods pretending to be a soldier, I loved life and was passionate about experiencing everything that I could. Of course at that time in my young state of growth I certainly didn't understand anything about the mind, how it worked, why it even worked the way it did, I just knew that my mind was extremely creative and wanted to be heard and seen in some way, even if it meant getting in trouble to express it. As I progressed through grade school into middle school the passion for creation and experience got stronger as well as my disdain for studies. I still did not want to do it, I felt like I did not fit into everyone else's version of normalcy that I saw in the children around me. The only classes that I truly took any pride and passion in were the ones that challenged my creative mind, whether it was art class, woodshop, music class or even agricultural classes for the sheer fact of getting to be outside. I was an energetic child, I loved martial arts and was a huge fan of Bruce Lee for a long time even into my adult life. As you are probably aware you certainly cannot excel just doing the work you enjoyed doing and blowing off the rest, I was good at that, so much so that I was failing the classes that would progress me through school. I ended up failing three separate times throughout my school years, getting held back while I watched my friends move up in their lives. If you have never felt that feeling, I can assure you it is a very deflating type of feeling. I do believe that failing played a big role in my confidence growing up and it certainly contributed to the actions I took that caused more self-harm than good. Although I failed school and got held back my father and stepmother were still there trying to get me through it. My father was the punisher while my stepmother was both the punisher and the lover, my father stepped in when he needed to but not too often, he deflected that on to her more than not. I played baseball for the local community team and I enjoyed that for many years into my teens. I have fond memories of being a pitcher and an outfielder, I was good at it, I enjoyed the physical activities of running and playing so of course I would enjoy sports to some degree. I also enjoyed the team aspect, again going back to a lack of cohesion at home being the only boy. I loved having the comradery of my teammates, it always made me feel accepted where in other aspects of life I may have felt like an outsider. I tried different sports throughout the years like track and football, but I wasn't really into them as much as baseball, that was the sport I enjoyed the most. I remember my father wanted so bad for me to play football that I eventually gave in and signed up for the local team. I played for one year and it wasn't even a full year for me, I had ended up at the bottom of a pile in practice one night and messed my leg up enough that I needed to be on crutches. That was it for me playing football, I didn't like it, I just did not like the impacts on my head and my body, it didn't seem natural to me. I believe there was part of me deep down inside that felt like I let my father down, like I was a disappointment to him because I couldn't live up to the boy he may have wanted or had envisioned for his "ideal son", I believe this may have played a role in my own lack of self-love in upcoming years. I made a lot of memories growing up in that town, riding my bike through the streets, the baseball field I played on was directly across from where we lived, the kids I used to play with in the neighborhood and even the half-house we lived in at the time. My sisters and I used to think it was haunted because we would hear things in the attic at night but I'm sure we were just being young and allowing what we watched at the time to influence our minds. There was one time my sister was so sure she woke up in the middle of the night and saw Rudolph the red nosed reindeer outside of her window she just wouldn't let it go, this was of course leading up to Christmas so naturally that's what was in our minds at the time, certainly now I understand the explanation of it but at the time it was exciting to think about especially with a huge imagination like mine. I loved living in that house, I loved our experiences together there, the tire swing, the environment around us in the neighborhood, it was all great for the time it served. I almost got ran over by a car being chased by the police one day while I was riding my bike, it's interesting to me how all of these memories are coming back in such detail but I remember that situation too, I almost feel like that car sped up intentionally to hit me as he blew through the alley way; thankfully I made it into our back yard just as the car sped past with the cop car speeding behind him. Looking back, I can honestly say that was the first of many times in my life that darkness will try and put an end to my human experience.

Life went on and the years passed as they tend to do, my father and stepmother ended were able to buy a house outside of town with some financial help from his father, and we ended up moving from our in-town setting to a more country atmosphere with farms and open spaces. I was just turning thirteen at the time and this was around the period where things in my life started to slowly take downward turn. Of course, I was still attending school, but I was older now and with an older crowd where the influence of being bullied and pushed around became more of an aspect in my life than in previous years. My stepmother was still doing everything she could to keep me on track with my schoolwork but that wasn't helping. She used to work closely with my teachers to ensure that every evening I was completing the assignments I needed to complete or the homework I needed to be doing was getting done, how tiring that must have been for her. My father and biological mother had a falling out before the move for reasons I'm not quite sure of, so she stopped coming around and my sister ended up moving to live with her a few hours north of us. This meant not having her around anymore in the house and feeling like more of an outsider in my own family. The section of the neighborhood we moved into was newly built, as was our newly built house but the openness of the location meant more alone time and more time to sit with my emotions. The house was beautiful two-story house that sat atop a hill with a long steep driveway, I always wondered why my dad would choose that type of location knowing the amount of snow we got in PA but it was his first house and I have no doubt he was proud of it. It's kind of funny looking back on it and I wonder to this day if anyone but me realized it but the house had a light gold siding with a deep red accent color on the shutters and the doors, being that my father's favorite football team was the San Francisco Forty-Niners I have a sneaky suspicion that was on purpose, although I never did ask about it. I loved that house as much as our previous home for the experiences that it provided me and my growth. Everything in life happens for us, not to us and this location provided experiences that were going to provide a path of learning in profound ways. We were around farms, open fields, and woods every day that we would frequent, and for a boy like me it was a great place to be.

As time went on I began making friends in the neighborhood and we had great times in that area, riding around the development we lived in, fishing in the nearby creek and playing in the nearby woods as well, but something in me started to change. I don't quite know if my actions were out of resentment for my mother not wanting to be around or if my failures in school and in sports made me feel like a disappointment but my relationship with my parents became more and more distant and I began to rebel against them and their rules. Maybe it was the music I was getting into that made me angry at the world, this neighborhood was where I met friends that first introduced me to playing instruments like guitar and drums and we would all get together at nights playing music in the kids outback shed. Someone close to me recently had said that confidence is the memory of success and if I apply that to life back then I immediately understand that I had no confidence in myself, I was living a life riddled with a lack of successes and music and art were what took my focus off of feeling like a failure. My father was a cigarette smoker for as long as I can remember growing up which led me to become curious and start picking up on that habit around this time as well. I was introduced to marijuana by some friends I made in the neighborhood and slowly began giving up on the things I enjoyed when it came to my creativity and the outdoors. That innocent little boy who was curious about the world and just wanted to explore and experience life creatively was fading away, becoming curious about the things that provided acceptance from others than from myself. I began masking and covering up my true essence and my true nature became diluted with falsehoods and agreements that I have made in my mind based on the environment around me at the time. I know that my performance in school was starting to really be affected by the way I was living and even certain teachers at times would reach out to try and help me. One teacher in particular I'll never forget was my art teacher, every time I was in her class I felt happiness, she influenced me in ways I wouldn't realize until later in life but she went out of her way to buy me art supplies, pencils, paper pads, even a big briefcase I could keep all my supplies in. She cared about me and my talents on such a deep level I am grateful for her existence every single day. I remember when I would go into her classroom, she would have incense burning and Enya playing softly on the radio, she is the reason why I still listen to Enya today and burn incense when I can. There were moments in school where I would be put into in-school suspension and she would walk in with art supplies to hand me, this way I would at least be utilizing my time wisely. I believe she is the one who ended up keeping all my artwork as well, I wonder what ever happened to her? Even though some people tried reaching out to help me I still was going to do whatever I wanted to do. As humans we label our decisions either "bad" or "good" but I now know that I was on a path for a reason, everything that had and was about to transpire in my life was setting me on a path towards enlightenment. A path of learning and growing through so many experiences and situations, they would lead me to finding myself sitting alone in Murfreesboro, Tennessee, reflecting on my current state of mind and looking back at all the circumstances I have had to struggle through in order to get to where I am today.

2. Tough Road Ahead

"SOME BEAUTIFUL PATHS CAN 'T BE DISCOVERED
WITHOUT GETTING LOST. " ~ EROL OZAN

While I became more and more independent in my thinking as a teenager, I also become more and more reckless in my choices. My mother had stopped coming around completely and my sister no longer lived in the household either. Feelings of abandonment started setting in and I couldn't quite figure out exactly what I did for my mother to stop wanting to see me. I think in some small way I started blaming myself, questioning what was wrong with me, combine that with the feelings of disappointment I felt about the son I was to my father, I was destined for the road that lay ahead. Someone had once told me that GOD does not use anyone in a godly way until he tests them deeply, and if that is true, he was about to be testing me deep. Back in those days I didn't believe in GOD nor did I have that type of regular influence in my life. I felt lonely, I began going through the emotions that nobody really cared about me and asking myself "what was the point of life anyway?" My actions became more and more sporadic and my parents certainly didn't know what I was going to do from one day to the next. I think they were just trying to keep things together with some semblance of normal, but deep down they were having a hard time keeping me in line.

There came a point where all the internal negative emotions began boiling over and taking control of my actions. The feeling that nobody cared about me started manifesting into my reality and I started thinking, if they don't care about me why should I care myself, which of course flowed over into everything I did. I began doing things like sneaking out of the house late at night or "running away" from home every chance I had, I use the quotation marks there because I never really went that far when I did runaway, combine that with alcohol and marijuana use, I was a mess and never even knew it. My school-work certainly didn't matter to me either, the only thing I cared about was hunting down and finding some sort of acceptance, whether it was with the wrong crowd or not, didn't matter to me, I just wanted someone to accept me. My decisions were certainly being made based on how many people I could get to like me or accept me for what I did or was willing to do. Even when it came to girlfriends, I didn't know what love was at that age, who does right, but for me it was all about who was giving me the attention that would attract me to them. I would make dumb decisions like pouring gun powder into a pile outside and lighting it with a lighter just to show off in front of friends, yeah, those kinds of decisions. I spent a little while without eyebrows or eyelashes after that one, I was glad to even have a face. There was also a time that I broke into a neighbor's house to steal a pair of rollerblades from their garage.

My friend had a pair back then and I didn't; I recall he wanted me to ride around the neighborhood with him but I couldn't, I also knew the girl in that particular house had a pair because I used to see her riding around with them. In this neighborhood, due to the location most families would leave there houses unattended with garage doors opened while they were away, yeah, that was too easy for me. The cops got called, I got in trouble and that turned out to be a learning experience in my life. Crazy thing about that whole situation is that I ended up marrying the girl I stole the rollerblades from in the future, interesting right? Yeah, my thoughts exactly.

One morning waking up for school I remember thinking to myself, what is the point, I was angry and unhappy at home, I felt lonely and unloved, I was constantly getting into trouble and I was taking my anger out on myself and my parents. I was giving up on me, not communicating to those around me how I felt, and I guess I needed to learn a lesson the hard way. This would come to me in the form of a unique gift from GOD as I like to call it. I look back on these situations today and can recognize the gifts they are but at the time it did not feel like a gift at all. This particular morning I was supposed to meet up with a friend of mine, who at the time was the only one of us who could drive and he was going to be taking a group of us to school that day. I left the house as I normally did, and we all piled in his car, what I didn't know at the time was the plan to skip that day of school, apparently, I didn't get that memo. Of course, I went along with the idea, I hated school anyway why would I want to be there around kids who just wanted to be bullies to me. I remember that to this day, it was early fall around September time frame, and we spent the day just riding around, probably wasted a whole tank of gas on the day, but it was fun indeed. We knew whose parents were working and which houses we could go to for a little to hang out throughout the day without getting caught. I had a girlfriend at the time who had chosen to come with us too, yep we were just a bunch of kids skipping school, smoking weed enjoying our freedom, that is exactly what it was, harmless freedom I thought.

Now the gift from GOD I had mentioned earlier. You see the plan for the day was that we would ride around burning up our time having fun. Along with knowing the details of empty houses to hang out in, we also knew the details of the school bus route and what times they typically drop off. We had it all planned out like some detailed military operation, where we would start taking kids back around the times the buses were to drop them off from school, keeping any suspicions under wraps that we missed that day of education. We made rather good time too doing it this way, but we failed to consider one tiny little detail, you see the school at that time had just started calling home when kids didn't show up in order to keep the parents aware, of course due to rampant kidnapping that was taking place at that time, as well as curbing truancy. Our bus stop was out of sight distance from my house and I was dropped off at almost the exact same time as the bus was pulling away from dropping the rest of the kids off in the neighborhood, I thought "nice, I'm in the clear, they'll never even know I skipped today." I was dead wrong, my parents did know, and they knew early in the morning, so they had all day to sit and think about the punishment they would hand down to me when I got home. I am fairly sure they had concerns that something could have happened to me, but I am also certain by the actions they took that day they were more focused on what they were going to do with me than my safety.

As I walked into the driveway leading up to the house I noticed at the front door sat trash bags full of stuff, not really taking in to account what they were I stepped past to go in the front door, that's when I was met at the door by my step-mother, who notified me that the bags contained all of my clothing and I was no longer accepted or allowed in the house and that I had to move out and figure it out for myself. I felt like my parents dumped me out like trash on the front stoop of their house, at the age of 16 for skipping school and I will be honest with you, this was the first time I ever skipped school, I may have blown it off and not cared but up until that point had never skipped. Don't get me wrong, I wasn't behaving in the best manner either but I could never in my wildest dreams think about doing that to my child no matter whom they were becoming or what they were doing. The implications this will have on the upcoming years of my life will send me into a whirlwind of overdoses, alcohol abuse, emotional instability, depression, and a hatred of self, moreover a loss of faith in myself and life. The ones I should have been able to trust the most threw me out that day like a bag of trash, a bag of trash I will carry around for years into my adulthood.

What is a 16 yr. old boy supposed to do when he is no longer accepted into his own family? When he is no longer allowed to live in the house that was meant to provide him with comfort? At the time I had no idea myself what I was going to do or how I was even going to handle this decision, so many emotions were flooding through me the day my parents kicked me out, I felt lost, rejected, hated, confused, I just couldn't understand what I did that was so wrong for everyone around me to not want me in their lives. I resented everyone, my mother didn't want to be around me anymore, at this point in my life I felt like my father was disappointed in me anyway for not being the boy he wanted, my stepmother was hard on us with the rules and responsibilities which, like I stated before I appreciate today, but at the time I felt like she hated me too. Where was this so-called GOD? Where was the magic that life was supposed to be about? I watched kids my age flourish in their lives, in school, in their family constructs, if there was a GOD why would he put me in a situation like this? I was so lost I didn't care if I lived or died anymore, I didn't care about school, I didn't care about myself, my health, my body, the rules, nothing, I just didn't care. Still standing on the stoop of my parents' house, the door closed and locked, the garage closed, it was just me in the middle of the world with a few bags of belongings trying to find in my mind some way to get myself out of this, I thought for a moment if I waited long enough they would start feeling bad and let me back in the house but by this time it was getting later in the day, I was hungry and in desperate need of some comfort, I needed somebody to help me.

My older sister and I always had a great relationship growing up, maybe just the fact that we were biologically related made us closer, it kept us in this mindset that we needed to look out for each other no matter what, even when the world was attacking us we needed to have each other's backs. By this time, her and my mother had a falling out as well, seems to be a pattern here of our parents not wanting us to be around. She lived with my mother for years before moving back to our hometown on her own. She was older, more responsible now, had a job, a fiancé, and a place to live. She seemed to be getting her things together and she was exactly the person I needed to reach out to. Standing there it finally hit me, I needed to call my sister. I walked across the street to the house I stole rollerblades from and where my future wife lived to ask them if I could use their phone. They gladly accepted me in and allowed me to make the call. They always were great folks even when I did wrong, they were nice people to me and I appreciate them for that, hell even after all my troubles growing up they allowed me to marry their daughter. I called my sister and told her what was happening, that our father and step mother were kicking me out of the house and I had nowhere to go, as I had expected she wasn't happy about it and made the 20 min drive to pick me and my belongings up to go live with her. I remember when she got to my father's house to grab me she had a few choice words for my parents, like I said my sister always had my back and was the one to be a lot more vocal about it than me. She made sure to let my parents know how she felt about them for what they have done to the both of us, here we were, two of my father's children forced out over the years. There was a huge piece of us both that felt like our stepmother was the one making all this happen, now she gets my father to herself and her daughter alone, certainly didn't help in the self-esteem department watching our father stand back allowing all this to happen to his children.

So, my sister had picked me up and taken me home to live with her and her fiancé, was it the best situation for a 16yr. old? No not exactly but the alternative certainly wasn't any better. Her and her fiancé were still young too, they didn't have any children and now I was their responsibility. They weren't ready for that either, but these were the cards we were dealt and neither one of them was going to let me to live on the street. She lived in town where I grew up too, so now I'm coming back into the streets that I used to ride bike as a little boy in, where a lot friends from school lived and I was with-in walking distance of the school. There was a lot more freedom to roam around and get into more trouble, which I certainly did, there were a lot of events that took place in a very short time span, almost too many to talk about. I was drinking and smoking a lot at this age, roaming the streets of town as often as possible, and I feel, in some small spiritual way, I was roaming around looking for answers to life not understanding what they could be. I began hanging around a good friend of mine who used to play guitar quite frequently, I would go to his house every day just to get a chance to sit and play on his guitars, it had a huge impact on my love of music later in life. I fell in love with playing the guitar, I was so into learning all the great bands of our time like Metallica, Slayer, Megadeth. We even got some drums at one point from a pawn shop and tried to form a little band, but I was in a bad spot to be even putting forth any effort for that type of commitment. This was also around the time that darkness was at work again trying to end my living experience. I would attend parties at friends' houses where there was always plenty of alcohol and marijuana, at the same time a few harder substances started showing up in my life at this time as well, like hallucinogens and cocaine, but alcohol always seemed to be there for me.

Now let me make this perfectly clear to the reader, I hated myself for where I was at in my life, for being lost, having no direction and no role model around to show me how to navigate through life or how to apply myself correctly in order to pull myself out of the situation I was in. I hated that my future looked grim, I used to say if I lived to the age of 25, I would be surprised, I guess someone heard me because I was about to put that thought to the test. One night while hanging out with some friends someone pulled out a bottle of whiskey, now at this time I hadn't really drank hard liquor, I mean I tried some over the years in a curious kind of way but not like I was about to consume it, beer was always the choice, probably because it was the easiest to get. I remember we were hanging out in the living room with loud music playing in the background, the room was as smoky as a local bar from all the cigarettes and I even recall the tv being on. I am not sure what overcame me that night but when I saw the full bottle, I knew I wanted it, I didn't care about the repercussions I just wanted to drink it. Now around the same time there were people piling into the gathering, which I guess by now you would call a party, and I remember someone handing me a joint to smoke. I enjoyed smoking marijuana, it was a great escape from the constant negative self-talk and the over-active thinking, so I gladly obliged. Unbeknownst to me this particular night the marijuana was "dirty", I mean it had cocaine in it, this being the first time I had ever done cocaine I had no clue what was about to happen to me. At first everything seemed normal, my heart was racing heavily, and I was extremely energetic. I clearly recall bouncing around the room being that goofy guy just wanting to be funny, nothing out of the ordinary for me I suppose. In comes the whiskey, like a thief to steal the night. Sitting on the kitchen counter, I clearly remember picking the bottle up, unscrewing the top and just putting it to my lips. I don't recall how much I consumed in a short period of time, but I clearly remember the ambulance ride to the hospital that night. I remember the medic who was frantically trying to save my life, funny thing was this guy happened to be someone I went to school with, talk about an awkward moment. I specifically remember him telling me that he was not going to let me die, he had my back; he certainly did too. I had overdosed on the cocaine and alcohol mixture, I remember the doctor telling me the next day how lucky I was to be alive and that they had to revive my heart that had stopped as well as pump my stomach from the liquor. In some way, looking back on these situations I can see that there was a battle between light and dark, a sort of spiritual battle taking place within me. Waking up in the hospital bed with family around me made me realize I needed to do something with my life, I needed help, deep down in my heart I knew I was made for better, I knew that little boy just wanted to be loved and allowed to show himself to the world. I needed someone or something to step in and save me, I needed and angel.

3. The Angels Amongst Us

"ANGELS ARE ALL AROUND US, ALL THE TIME,
IN THE VERY AIR WE BREATHE."
~ EILEEN ELIAS FREEMAN

As I stated in the previous chapter I never really believed in GOD, I didn't believe in the spiritual forces that surround us nor was I aware of how the bible was actually an allegory to the battle we all deal with on our journey into conscious awakening. Through the years of studying and practicing I have come to learn a lot about my situations and how they were meant to happen for me at exactly the right moments in time. I have gained a new understanding for the infinite intelligence but that didn't come easy. I was meant to go through what I went through in order to get here, I understand that the more we fail to listen and see the signs along our journey, the further detached we become from our true essence, or our true purpose in life. In my case someone, something, some spiritual nature needed to step in and guide me back onto the path that would bring me to this awakening if were to happen in this lifetime, and wouldn't you know it, the angel I was looking for had been in my life the whole time. Now there have only been a select few individuals in my life that I consider to be "heroes", those individuals that I just admired with unwavering commitment, here as of recent the life coach that I had the pleasure of meeting has become one of those individuals but the one most important person in my life I consider my hero was my grandmother Elsie. I loved and admired her for the way she loved others, her commitment to love was done in such a way I still have trouble putting it into words, she was absolutely an amazing woman. I believe in angels and in the infinite intelligence that surrounds us, she was certainly the angel I needed and the one who was going to save my life.

After being discharged from the hospital I remember my father was the one who wanted to take me home to his house, after all this time of him kicking me out, driving by me on the streets of town waving and continuing on like I was just another every day citizen, he wanted to take me back home. You would think that I would be excited, that I would be happy to be with my father again in the house that I loved being in but I wasn't, I was actually angry about it, I had emotions running through me still from what he had done to shut me out, for not being there for me and building a father son relationship with me, for making me feel like I wasn't good enough, but now that I almost died he wants to step in. I allowed him to take me back to his house, I guess out of curiosity as to how things may have changed in the home, maybe a little bit of being nosey I suppose, but when we got there it was a little awkward. There was no one else home, my step-sister was in school and my step-mother was at work, my dad stated he needed to go to bed because he had to work that night and needed some sleep, and all of a sudden just like that I was alone again, sitting in his basement room on the couch just released from the hospital after almost dying, I sat alone. Of course, I wasn't having that, there was no way was I going to allow this to happen to me again, no way was I going to sit in this house feeling those feelings again like I was a disappointment and no one wanted to be around me. So, I picked up my fathers' phone and called a friend in town to come pick me up, and they most certainly did, girlfriend and all. While my father was asleep I was leaving his house to go back into the town where this all started, the only difference this time was that I was going to make some changes that would have an impact on my life forever, or so that's what I told myself. I still had episodes where I bounced around from my sisters, to my aunt's house, back to my sister's house, getting in trouble, stealing cars, smoking cigarettes, so many people tried to have a hand in helping me find my way but to no avail. There would be another episode during this time where I would be rushed to the hospital for overconsuming alcohol before an angel took over and finally set me on the correct path.

Sitting at my sister's house one day I started contemplating ways that I thought would better serve me and my future, the first thing I wanted to do was drop out of high school. Time had gone by now and I was 17yrs old and by law I was an emancipated adult, all I needed to do was talk to my guidance counselor and that was a done deal but how would I proceed in life without a high school diploma was the dilemma I faced, but I did it anyway. Here I was at 17yrs old, I had been in the hospital twice now and almost died from irresponsible behavior, and just quite school, I needed to do something. In steps my grandmother, like the beautiful savior that she was, out of the blue she came to my sister's house after I had dropped out and stated that she wanted me to come live with her. Now my grandmother was always around in our lives, she was close to my father and we would see her all the time but we weren't really close, everyone kept telling me I was her favorite but up until this point I hadn't realize it. She was a deeply religious woman who always wanted to preach to you about Jesus and the bible, sometimes it got on my nerves but that was just the ego in me talking. I hesitated at first mainly because as a 17yr old I had too much pride, who wants to live with their grandmother you know, she was old, that would be boring etc.… all those immature things that teenagers would say about someone like that, I said them to myself. Something in me agreed though, that deep down desire to do better for myself took over and I packed all my things and moved in with her. She took me in and immediately loved on me, she fed me, made me homecooked meals every day and showed me what it felt like to be accepted by someone again, to feel loved by someone on a deep level, she was saving my life one day at a time with her love.

While living with her I was still a little unsure of what I wanted to do in life but she really helped guide me along, she helped me get my first job at a tire place in town changing tires for the community, she took me to the local dealership and helped me get my first car. I was able to get my license, but I still needed a plan though, now I was 17 and no longer in school, I was working changing tires and time was certainly not going to stop. Without my knowledge my grandmother had gone and purchased a GED study book, she had intentions herself for me and my future that I was unaware of at the time. For the next month, every night she would force me to study for my GED, she would quiz me and ask me questions, she really took the time to help me prepare for the test. The time came and we scheduled the exam at the local community college, I remember being so nervous on the ride up there I thought for sure I was going to fail. I still hadn't had any confidence in myself but I went anyway, sat down and took that long test, I just kept thinking in my mind "please let me pass this, I need better for my life, please." Sure enough about two weeks later I received a phone call from the college, I still remember the way the lady told me too, she said "Hello Mr. Spigelmeyer, I'm calling in regards to the test you had taken for your GED (long forever pause), the pause felt like it drug on for days, but she continued "I was just calling to tell you congratulations, you passed and will be awarded your diploma in a few days' time." Victory!! I had my first victory in such a long time, I can't explain to you the feelings of accomplishment that flooded over me, it felt like a huge weight was lifted off my shoulders, this opened up so many doors and paths to a better life and I was happier than I had been in quite a long time. I still had moments with my grandmother where I would go out and smoke weed with friends, but I respected her rules, I respected the time she wanted me to be home and I obeyed her and came home, high or not I still came home to her. I don't think there was anything she wouldn't do for me or allow me to do so long as I was safe. The apartment she lived in at the time only had enough room for her and I but she still allowed me to set up a drum set at one point in her bedroom, she was such a wonderful part of my life and an important part of my growth.

I was so happy that I had opened the door that I did with my GED, it felt like I could do anything now, absolutely anything I wanted to do was possible in my life with that diploma. I actually come from a line of individuals who had spent their lives serving in the military, an uncle of my fathers, my mother's father had served in the Army, my sister's boyfriend was actually a recently separated 82nd Airborne paratrooper and my aunts husband at the time was in the Army, pair that with my childhood story of playing in the woods pretending to be in the Army, a strong urge came over me to join the military. I had my GED now and there just happened to be a recruiting station right in town at that time, why not go have a conversation with those guys, I knew this would get me out of town and that's what I needed more than anything. I remember talking this over with my grandmother and immediately I could see the worry in her face, she had a particular view on the military and the dangers that came with serving that I don't think she was very fond of the idea but this is what I loved about her, she wanted me to be happy, she wanted me to pursue whatever dream I may have had whether she herself liked it or not, she wouldn't stand in my way. So that's what I did, I walked in to town and sat down with the Army recruiters to talk about my options, of course there was a process and the fact that I didn't have my actual GED in hand yet I had to wait until that came, which was good because it gave me time to study for the ASVAB exam, the military entrance exam. Time came and went, I received my diploma, my grandmother again helped me study and I went and took that exam, based off my score I had options of being an ordnance guy loading howitzer cannons or an infantryman, I wasn't able to go active duty yet because of my score but everything happens for a reason and you'll discover that reason here shortly. I chose to be a howitzer guy, the idea of driving tanks around sounded so awesome to me, plus I was only going National Guard so if things were too much or I didn't like it I wasn't somewhere over seas, I would still be at home with grandma. The excitement I had inside me for this new adventure in my life was unexplainable, the pain I felt over the years from my parents, the feelings of being a failure and not feeling good enough were slowly dissipating, I know they were still there in an underlying sense but I felt good again, I felt like things were getting better for me and I had a direction to my life. The future that lay ahead was uncertain, but it was certainly better than what I had previously thought it was going to be. After my military entrance exam there was a period where I had to wait until all my training started and I got shipped off to bootcamp. During this time, I had reconnected with a girl that I knew from high school and we ended up getting pretty close, we dated for a little while and she ended up getting pregnant, not what I was planning to have happen but it happened nonetheless. She had the baby girl but our relationship didn't work out, she didn't want to be with someone who would be gone all the time and I understood that but I wasn't staying in that town any longer, sometimes sacrifices need to be made in order for big changes to occur and I needed a big change. There were moments of drama where she wanted me to have no involvement in the child's life, but wanted me to pay support for her, which I never argued, I was tired of being a disappointment and I certainly wasn't going to shirk that responsibility. The time came for me to leave town and embark on a journey that was best for everyone involved, even them.

I was embarking on a journey into unknown territory. The day I was set to leave for Ft. Sill, Oklahoma was a memorable day for me indeed as my family was all there to see me off. Yes my father and step-mother both showed up to see me off along with all the others who had helped me along my path, my sister, my aunt and my grandmother all came to the airport to watch me board the plane for bootcamp. There were so many firsts for me now, the first time I'd ever been on a plane, the first time I'd ever been out of the state of PA, the first time I had to have the courage to go out into the world and leave my family behind all by myself, I was so scared that day getting on the plane I remember just telling myself "if now is the time I die than so be it, at least I made it this far and all my family was here to see it." I was leaving that old life behind, those old feelings of not being good enough, those old feelings of depression and the need to mask them with substances like alcohol and drugs, I was off to becoming something different, something and someone of meaning and I was excited beyond belief. I gave my final hugs to everyone and walked down the pathway, gave one final look back then boarded the plane. I found my seat by the window and watched as the flight attendant closed the door and got everyone ready for takeoff. As the plane taxied to the runway, I remember seeing my family all lined up standing at the windows watching the plane, so many emotions flooded through me, this was really happening, I was really flying away, no turning back even if I wanted to. We got to our takeoff line and I listened as the plane's engines came up on power, the sound was amazing, so loud, so powerful, what an experience for me. I felt the brakes release and was thrust back into my seat, in an instant I was gone, adrift in the sky like a feather in search of a better me, in search of a better and bigger purpose in this life. Little did I know, one of those demons got on the plane that day and would come to have a heavy hold on me for many years to come.

4. Breaking the Mold

"THE SECRET OF CHANGE IS TO FOCUS ALL OF YOUR ENERGY,
NOT ON FIGHTING THE OLD, BUT ON BUILDING THE NEW."
~ SOCRATES

A 30,000-foot view of the world was a brand-new perspective for me. This journey that I had embarked on at a young age, was one that will profoundly impact the change in me that was inevitable. I believe in the idea that circumstances are presented to us throughout our lives to teach us and help us grow in our self-love and unity, providing the opportunity to learn and become better versions of ourselves but only if we choose to pay attention. As I stated in previous chapters it is apparent to me now that I was being guided down a particular road for a reason, to learn as much as I could learn about life, love and emotions, in order to teach through my experiences and have a positive impact on the lives of others. Joining the military, in my opinion was the greatest decision I had ever made. Not only did I build relationships, but I was introduced to the world, to travelling, to different cultures and to a plethora of knowledge right at my fingertips. Core values that I had not gained while in small town PA were instilled in me and I started to really learn the value of qualities like, leadership, loyalty, duty, service to others and integrity. It wasn't an easy road to venture down but I can assure you it was better and far more beneficial to, not only me, but those I would come to serve in the future.

Landing at the Oklahoma City Airport I had absolutely no clue what I had gotten myself in to. I was alone, nervous, excited yet scared and all I kept thinking to myself was, "well they can't kill me, so just do what you are told to do and you'll be fine", that was my pep-talk to myself, do what you are told and you will either make it or not make it, those are the only two possible outcomes. I was picked up at the airport by a shuttle and taken to a nearby hotel where others who were waiting to go to bootcamp also had rooms. "Finally," I thought, I get to interact with others who were my age, sharing the same nervous emotions, it took some of the stress off and allowed me to focus on other conversations than the ones I was having with myself. We were left in the hotel for the night with instructions to be ready for the bus to pick us up the next morning. We were all nervous and excited all the same, but we didn't waste any time getting our last cigarettes in or even last few beers in our system, we knew (or so we thought) that lifestyle was about to end. The next morning came and the bus arrived on time just like they said it would, three gentleman with wide brimmed hats and army uniforms stepped off the bus, one had a clipboard of names, while the other two began helping us get our things together ensuring we had what we needed in our bags. They all seemed extremely nice and my immediate thought was, "wait, if they are this nice to us, bootcamp is going to be a cakewalk", remember, I had no clue what I was talking about at the time. We loaded up our bags on our backs and began filing on the bus until everyone was comfortable and situated, the three-gentleman took their seats at the front of the bus and off we went. We all talked to each other but the guys in uniform weren't talking at all, I remember sitting back and thinking "wow look how sharp these guys are in their uniforms, you mean I get to be like this? How exciting." I don't remember many details of the bus ride but I certainly remember leading up to a set of train tracks that day and how those three gentleman flipped like a light switch on all of us once we crossed over. As we approached the tracks, the first guy stood up and began telling us exactly how we were to get off the bus once we arrived, how we were not to be looking them in the eyes and how we were to be focused on what we are told to do when we get off the bus, his demeanor was a lot more forceful this time and I started getting a little more worried at this point. Then the bus stopped at the tracks, like most busses do, this had to be their signal to each other because as soon as he closed that door and proceeded across, the other two stood up and hell was unleased inside that bus. I don't even remember what they were screaming but each was yelling something different, telling us how to sit, how to be looking, how not to be looking, extreme confusion and loudness that day, now I was scared!

Bootcamp was an awesome experience for me, and I wouldn't change the opportunity for the world. I did so many things there and in my specialized training that turned me into a better man, that forced me to grow up quick. I made so many friends there and so many memories at that moment in my life, I can't help but love looking back and remembering those days, remembering those experiences and how they shaped me for so much better in my life. My existence up to this point had been full of disappointment, I had carried myself around every day thinking I was nothing, I was worthless and that nobody cared about me but that all changed there in Fort Sill, Oklahoma; I finally found a group of people who cared, a group of men and women who helped me through tough times, that I helped through obstacles, we helped each other and we all were willing to die protecting one another, I never felt that feeling before in my life and I loved every minute of it. Some people talk about how they had negative feelings towards basic training, how they didn't like their drill sergeants etc... but for me, that comradery was all that I needed to have the time of my life. Every waking day there was fun for me, we were running around carrying guns, climbing obstacles, learning new skills, camping out, playing war, I felt like that little boy and his curiosity had returned to me again. Unfortunately this was also around the time that my mother's father had passed away, I remember the chaplain coming to me and telling me that my grandfather had passed and asking if I would want to fly home for his funeral, which I did regardless of how little I knew him. At the funeral and the burial, I was told a little more about him, how he was a lover of country music, playing guitar and singing as well as running in marathons. They told me he had a form of cancer and needed to amputate his legs, or he'd die, he refused to allow the operation to happen telling my grandmother "they aren't taking my legs." The amount of guts that takes to stare death in the face without fear and go headfirst like he did, still amazes me to this day, he knew the result of that decision. I believe I brought part of him back with me after that, after hearing those stories and hearing them play taps when they laid him in the ground, I came back to bootcamp more determined than ever to be awesome at what I did, to have the strength to just push through whatever was thrown my way. In a crazy kind of way, I get the feeling GOD wanted me to go there, he wanted me to hear about him and who he was, and just how strong one could truly be, he wanted to meet him one last time, for me.

After my time at basic training and my specialized job training in OK, I was sent back to my National Guard unit in PA where I would serve for roughly a year before venturing off again into another sphere of the military. Now I always talk about synchronicities and how they are divine communications to us, some say to remind us that we are on the right path, or I've heard others say they are there to guide us if we truly pay attention but at this stage in my life I knew nothing about them and it's only through growth and reflection that I am able to see them shown in my past. Upon returning to Pennsylvania to serve my guard unit I got my job back at the tire place in Elizabethtown and returned to live with my grandmother again during this time. Life was good, things were looking up for me as I was working, saving money, and aspiring to go active duty for the Army. I would go to work, come home, and spend time with my grandmother while getting to have time with my buddies on the weekends for duty. Remember that little demon I mentioned in the last chapter that hopped on that plane, well he started making his presence known to me around this time as well. I was in the Army now, I was grown I thought, I could make good decisions, right? Well every time we had drill or when I was with my buddies, we used that excuse to drink beer. It was nothing out of the ordinary to go out in the field for the weekend with coolers full of beer, harmless right? Let us just remember that. A couple of us had come up with this grand idea of wanting to go into the special forces of the Army, we wanted to be the best of the best, which was a huge change from where I was not so long ago in that town. I had been working out now with my friends, I was getting bigger, stronger, more confident and less fearful of the bad things that could happen to me, of course grandma hated the idea, but again wanted me to be happy and I was motivated to just accomplish something big. We all talked about going into the Army Rangers at first but finally concluded that if we were going to be the best, we would need to be Navy SEALS. I used to enjoy running long distances and still do to this day while listening to SEAL cadence, there was always something about it that I just loved, it kept me in step with them and made me feel like a badass. So here's where the future proves the past, my buddies and I decided that's what we were all going to do, we put in transfer packages to our command and applied for the U.S. Navy under the SEAL program they had at the time, a transfer from one service to another was possible if a program was offered in one that the other didn't offer. Everything got accepted and we just had to wait until the time came for us to get shipped off to Navy bootcamp, yes, I had to go through another bootcamp, but this one surprisingly wasn't nearly as challenging. While waiting I happened to attend a gathering at a family members house one night and as it happens I bumped into the girl from my old neighborhood who I had stolen the rollerblades from, remember that gem of a story, well we got to talking and reconnecting, come to find out she was waiting to go into the Navy also. Wow what a coincidence right? Well we ended up talking, getting close and falling for each other. We decided that the only way we would be able to stay together was if we went into the Navy already married, they would not separate us then. So that's what we did, we went to the local justice and got married Nov 21st 1998 and that is how I ended up in the Navy, married to the hometown girl that I had stolen from and would end up having children with. I have a firm belief that GOD is always in control, there are no coincidences, and these events were taking place for me and my growth in to awakening.

We ended up going to Navy bootcamp together as a married couple, which wasn't the best simply for the hell we both got thrown at us just for being married and being there together, the drill sergeants knew and Spigelmeyer become a popular phrase in the chow hall. I never made it into the Navy SEAL program, I'm sure for many reasons, I had a wife now and was thinking about a family, I still had negativity inside my mind that made me a quitter at times too, but regardless, as I always say things happen for a reason and I have no regrets whatsoever. My wife and I had some pretty rough times being married inside the Navy environment, we lost our first child Cobi to the unfortunate, I guess natural event of the umbilical cord choking him, we found this out one month before he was due to be born. That hit us both pretty hard, we didn't stop though, we ended up having two more beautiful children who are growing up to be magnificent human beings, but with the loss of Cobi came more drinking for me. The military life puts a lot of stress on young married couples and we split up a few times throughout the years trying to make things work with one another. Our very first deployment together being a young married couple should have been a sign for me, but I failed to pay attention. I had left my young wife alone in San Diego while I went out and explored the world, going into countries like Hong Kong, Malaysia, Singapore, Bahrain, Dubai, Australia, I was having the time of my life drinking and partying, while she was left at home to take care of things alone. Coming back from that deployment, I came home to an empty house, while I was living it up, she was struggling, and I wasn't there to comfort her through it. Those lonely feelings were taking over again, those feelings of being abandoned started coming back and I didn't know how to deal with them, so I resorted to what I knew best, alcohol. I bought myself a bottle of 100 proof liquor that night and proceeded to drink the whole thing. I remember talking to my sister on the phone while drinking that night but not much after that, she called the ambulance from PA to SD and they came to the house and forced their way in to save me, again. This is now the third time I had gone to the hospital because of my self-sabotage, when was I going to learn? We ended up reconciling our differences and getting back together but like I said we would end up going through a couple more break ups over the years that would take their toll on us both. Now I must be careful to not paint a picture of everything in my life being terrible, we did have good times together and we made wonderful memories living on the west coast and the east coast. We did a ton of things as a family at the beaches, museums and amusement parks but my underlying pain from the past was never dealt with and had continued to come out more and more and the years passed by. I am most certainly thankful for those times and for the path they led me down.

Now the whole time while I was in the military my grandmother was always reaching out to me, she was still a positive influence in my life, and I would visit her every time I went home on leave. I remember she would always say to me "Timmy, you need to get out of the military and come home to me." She was serious about that too, if I would have gotten out and moved back to PA she would have been as happy as could be. She missed me, she genuinely loved me, and was the only one in my life who has ever made me feel truly loved, still to this day I've never found anyone who accepted me the way she had. When I had gotten out of Navy bootcamp and gone home on leave she had given me her credit card so that I could drive from PA to CA all by myself, which by the way I never want to do again; alone anyway. She was just that type of person and the day I lost her will be a day I will never forget. I was stationed in VA Beach at the time, my wife and I had our little family unit and we were doing ok, I was still drinking, I was attending school for Visual Communications and on shore duty, she was in school for her RN degree and everything was as good as it could be for the time. I remember receiving a call from my grandmother one Friday night and she was adamant about me coming home, she really wanted to see me, she missed me. She begged me to drive up to PA for the weekend and spend some time with her, but I didn't. I found every excuse in my mind as to why I couldn't make that drive, but mostly because I was selfish, I was more worried about me than I was about the only one who ever really cared about me. Looking back, I can only imagine how that broke her heart, me saying no, me blowing her off like she meant nothing to me. I received a call the next day that she had died, she had a heart attack and was gone. Just like that I felt an immense regret in my life, I couldn't believe what I had done to her, part of me felt like I did that to her, that if I would have just visited her maybe she would've been okay, maybe I broke her heart and she couldn't go on. That killed me, I had a hard time dealing with the loss of my grandmother, for years I beat myself up about it and the drinking started to get progressively worse. I played a song I had written for her at her funeral, I would go to her grave and write her notes stuffing them in the ground at her tombstone, or I would just sit there for hours telling her I was sorry, I would've done anything to have another chance to tell her I love her, to thank her for all she had done for me in my life to lead me down the path I was on, I probably wouldn't be here if it weren't for her and I never told her that. I hated myself again after that and I was most certainly about to show it through my actions.

I was slowly getting back into bad habits again when it came to drinking alcohol which was having a negative effect on my marriage. I began closing off, I started to feel lost again, those old feelings started coming back to me without my grandmother and I had no control over myself. We divorced in 2010 and she moved back to PA with the boys, leaving me alone in VA Beach, now the lonely feeling was different though, I was a father who was alone without his boys and I didn't have the one person in the world who made me feel like I could get through anything, I felt like I had no one to rely on again. I couldn't stand any of these emotions, my drinking was getting out of control which resulted in disciplinary action taken against me from the Navy. I had always had a great career up to that point, I was a stellar performer who won awards and accolades, I was junior sailor of the year, I was a leading petty officer, I was always proud of what I had done but I couldn't control myself anymore when it came to my feelings mixed with alcohol. My time spent in the Navy was full of awesome experiences in which I was able to learn and expand my mind on so many levels. It seemed when I was, there was a huge push for everyone to just learn as much as they could and up until this, I did, and I loved every minute of it. I ended up getting out of the Navy and moving back to PA on December 21st, 2010 under a general discharge for problems with alcohol. I could have stayed in and had an okay enough career without my wife and kids, but my grandmother passing was too much for me, the world wasn't the same without her in it. I didn't understand anything anymore nor was I even sure who I was, I lost confidence in myself again and all those old feelings from my past were coming out into the world around me. I remember at one point asking myself why it seemed that I destroyed everything around me that I loved the most, I blamed myself for every single thing that had ever happened in my life when all along the lesson I was being taught was actually about loving and accepting myself, something I wouldn't grasp for years to come.

5. Coming Home

"MY HOME WILL NEVER BE A PLACE, BUT A STATE OF MIND." ~ CHARLOTTE
ERIKSSON

My departure from the military after 12 years of service was both bittersweet as well as disappointing. I had gone through so many trials and tribulations in my life that serving in the military was my saving grace as far as victories were concerned. This was the place that shaped me, the institute that took a broken young boy with zero confidence and molded him into a strong, independent, and powerful thinking man. I just could not believe that after all this time I was getting out and not in the way that I had envisioned in my mind. It was always a joke within my inner circle that I would retire in the Navy. I was disappointed in myself for my actions towards the end of my career, for reverting backwards to old ways with drinking and self-sabotage, and the depression that I was about to face was the worst I'd ever felt. December 21st 2010 was the date I was scheduled to depart the Navy and I had no clue what I was going to do, I had no direction, worst of all my grandmother was no longer here. How was I going to face my family after getting out the way that I did, would they even really care? It always felt like the military was a coattail for them to grab hold of and use for bragging rights, they never came to my graduations, they never visited me where I was stationed, but they sure did tell everyone how "proud" they were of me. The next ten years of my life would lead me to an awakening that I am so thankful for, a strength in myself that I thank GOD for every single waking day.

I was drinking heavily by this time and smoking a lot too, when I say I felt lost I really mean, I felt lost. I was all alone in the house we used to live in just waiting until it was time to move back north, everywhere I looked was a reminder of my family, I missed my kids, I missed being a father and a husband, I was willing to cling to anything that came my way and alcohol was my main crutch. I was drinking so much as this point that my mind was in a fog, like there was no sense of making the right decisions for myself. Once I moved back I needed a plan as to what I was going to do for employment, the military mindset in me thought that I needed to do something that would make me a valuable asset anywhere in the U.S, so getting my class A CDL was the route I would end up taking. I moved in with a woman I knew from school, but that was just me wanting to fill the void of losing my family, I had no idea what I was doing, I certainly wasn't in love, hell I just wanted to survive each day at this point. I enrolled in the local community college to get my CDL training and finished that training shortly after. Following school I became an over the road truck driver for a company in Iowa and began down a path of finally pulling myself together financially and getting some stability under my feet again although I was still an emotional wreck from the divorce, losing my grandmother and getting out of the military the way I did. I was told I displayed signs of PTSD and that I should go to the VA about it, which I did but the medication wasn't for me, I didn't like the feeling so I stopped them after the first day or so. I preferred alcohol and that didn't show signs of going away any time soon.

I ended up coming off the road and getting a local truck driving job, the loneliness of being out there was not doing me and my emotions any good. Every chance I got I was drinking, not while driving, but when I stopped for the night I would go into the bar, the club or the store and buy alcohol. Living back in PA was allowing me to reconnect with my family again, my father and I were talking a lot more now but he was still the same person I had known growing up, there wasn't much I was going to do about that and deep down inside I held resentment for what he had done to me at a young age, which did come out on him one drunken night too. I hadn't reached the point of forgiveness yet and all the drinking I was doing wasn't going to allow those feelings to go away. I was getting to visit my grandmothers grave on a regular basis, as well as my son Cobi's, I remember her wish was to be buried right beside him when she passed and she was, her and my son are buried in the same graveyard beside each other in my hometown. I was getting a chance to reconnect with some old friends I hadn't seen in a long time, most of them in the bars while I was drinking. I was putting on weight from all the alcohol and I was becoming angry and taking it out on the people around me. I was 35yrs old, working as a local truck driver, spending most of my income at the bar every night drinking and shooting pool. This was the norm for many of the people I knew, they worked and went out to the bars, but this probably wasn't a good idea for someone who struggles with alcohol abuse. I was never labeled an alcoholic, but I was told by the military physicians and psychologists that I was an alcohol abuser, which would come full circle to almost killing me yet again. My depression, loneliness, emptiness, and feelings of being lost were out of hand. I used to carry a shotgun shell in my pocket to remind myself where I was at emotionally, every time I touched it was a reminder to me about what state I was in and how quickly I could end it if I wanted to. I was drinking to the point of blacking out while driving and I remember a particular night of being at the bar where I was just pounding drinks, I don't know what the anger was about, but I was just throwing them back. I remember leaving to drive home and being woke up by my father pulling me out of my truck, which he spotted in a field on his own way home. I had blacked out driving, swiped somebody's mailbox and ended up in the middle of a cornfield. I can't express enough how thankful I am that I didn't hurt anyone and how happy I am to be alive today.

I know looking back that my grandmother never would have approved of the way I was treating myself and she would have stepped in immediately. One night while drinking at a local bar I ended up meeting an interesting woman. We ended up getting together and dating for only a short while, but she did something to me while we were together. She introduced me to things that started to make impressions into my subconscious mind. She had lost her husband to an accident a few years prior to us meeting from alcohol, so she herself was dealing with inner emotions and demons. We both were drinking quite a bit, but at the same time she had wisdom in her, an almost ancient type of wisdom. She began talking to me on a spiritual level and introducing me to books by the likes of Thich Nhat Hanh, Deepak Chopra, Don Miguel Ruiz and Neville Goddard. She began talking to me about meditation and spirituality on a level that I never even heard of before. She would have vivid dreams at night, then share them with me the next day in such a powerful way I was moved by her stories. She had told me that marijuana was a cure for alcoholism at one point which piqued my curiosity. Even though I was in the state I was, there was always a deep down burning feeling that knew I was better, I knew I was great but I didn't know how to show it, I didn't know how to shine like I was supposed to. She would end up becoming the turning point in my life that would bring me to the spiritual awakening I am in today, her passion for the subject was intriguing to me and whether I fully grasped it at the time or put the practices in place, she planted the seeds in my mind that would later become the most fruitful pieces of information I had ever received. Our relationship didn't end up working out, which was, in all reality, the way it was meant to be, I was just clinging to people out of the fear of being alone. I began smoking marijuana now and began feeling more control over myself, as it turns out the alcohol slowly started disappearing from my life. I was still an emotional mess from all the years of shit I endured but for some strange reason this was helping. Time went on and the years would pass by and wouldn't you know it the alcohol just up and walked away from me, crazy I know but I started to lose the taste for it. Yeah, I was smoking weed and getting stoned every day when I got home from work, but I was safe. I wasn't hurting anyone, and, in all actuality, I started to become more curious about things, like reading, playing more music and just being more creative. The marijuana had come back in to my life at just the right moment, say what you will about it but with responsible daily use this stuff had just taken away the one thing that I had clung on to for years, the one thing that had destroyed me for years was just all of a sudden an afterthought, I still can't explain it.

Years would go by and I would end up falling again for a woman whom I adored, and we would blend our families together. She had two boys and my two boys would visit every other weekend, things were certainly a lot better for me and my future by this time. Every now and then the pains and emotions from the past would come back in certain situations and I think I was still taking things out on the people around me but it wasn't nearly what it was just a few years earlier. I was smoking marijuana quite frequently now, but it was helping me on so many levels, I didn't want to stop. Let me be clear for one second and say that this is not a promotion for the use of marijuana at all, it helped me when I needed it the most and as of today I no longer require the use of any substances in my body like that. I decided to use my G.I. Bill and go back to school to get my bachelor's in music production and spent the entirety of our time together trying to fulfill a tiny goal I had in my mind for my grandfather. Let me take a step back for a moment and bring my mother's father into the picture again. I stated to you earlier that my grandfather would end up having an impact on my life even though I didn't really know him all that well. You see he was a guitar player and I knew that growing up from the little visits we got to have with him, I never got to hear him play but I knew that he played because I always saw his guitar and microphone stand in his bedroom. He would never play for us and I never got to hear him until later in life when I was attending a gathering with some family members. My stepbrother had some cassette tapes my grandfather had recorded and put them in the tape player. Immediately I was blown away, I couldn't believe this man had never played for us. I was told that he was shy and didn't have the confidence to play in front of people which is why we never got to hear him play growing up. That had an emotional impact on me, he was great at it but never showed it to the world because of his lack of confidence and I could relate. I felt that I needed to honor him in some form or fashion, I started facing my own fear of playing guitar and singing in front of people to the point that I would build up my own confidence in the act. That was how I started the image of J.R. Lee Music, I utilized his first and last name initials and my middle name to form the stage name I would use to play around for people in PA. I always said that was how I took him out and got him to live his dream of playing for crowds. The impact this small accomplish will have on my own self confidence would end up shaking my whole world and attracting opportunities into my life I never would've expected. I enjoyed being creative again, playing music, having a family, being a husband a father again but man, when GOD has a plan for you, he truly has a plan and will shift the entire universe around in order to ensure that plan is put in to place.

We spent four years together before getting married in September 2018 and during our time together I began getting deeper into reading and researching meditation and yoga. The knowledge I was picking up through these books was beginning to have an impact on my thinking and the way I view the world around me. I became interested in the subconscious mind through books I stumbled upon in college and how the effects of sound resonance could heal us of traumas. I would go to sleep at night listening to solfeggio frequencies and positive affirmations, whilst getting in the habit of writing affirmations in the mornings in a journal I kept beside my bed. I created a company called "The Creative Mind Media" after reading a book stating how we are all connected to the one creative mind, or GOD. I began practicing yoga and meditation daily, I made it part of my morning and nighttime rituals to sit in silence. As I was putting all this effort into these practices, I had no idea what it was doing internally to my mind, body and spirit. There were moments in time where I remember reading certain books and crying because of the profound realization I was having at that very moment. I was starting to have deep visions during my meditations that were influencing me and my views of the world around me. I would try to explain to everyone in my life what was happening to me but they would never quite understand, they never really understood what I meant when I told them I talked to GOD in meditation and came out of it completely rattled, my body shaking or how I had a vision of my son talking to me before receiving a phone call from his mother explaining to me how he said exactly the same thing to her the night before. Something was happening to me on a spiritual level and no one around me understood. I would meditate and speak to my grandmother, I feel like I finally got to tell her how I felt, and these weights were being lifted off my shoulders every single day that I continued practicing. I remember running through the house after a particular meditation, going into every room telling everyone what just happened to me and what I saw. Of course, they all looked at me like I was crazy, but I remember being so shaken that I couldn't even sit still. Ok ok, I will tell you this one because it was exceptionally profound for me. I made it a habit to meditate in the morning and in the evening, regardless of what was going on I always tried to make time for it. This night I remember getting my space ready for meditation by using sage and clearing out the negative energy in the room. I would then light candles, and incense and turn the lights out so that it was completely dark in the room. Now, I would use solfeggio music during meditation because it's a natural resonance and has the power to really tap into your brain powers and the natural vibrations of the universe. As I got into the meditation I remember clearly floating out into space, I was hovering above the earth and I had a 360-degree view all around me. I could see all through space as I looked around, the stars, the sun, the planets, it was amazing, I felt like I was in space, I even felt that sinking feeling I would get when flying on a plane. As the meditation went on, I slowly began drifting away from the Earth, out into the infinite universe. I know it sounds strange but just bear with me. As I'm floating away, watching the planet get smaller and smaller I began passing other planets and stars, I even saw space dust, it was a crazy feeling but I eventually saw a bright white light that I got closer and closer to. I began to feel like I was being drawn towards this light for some reason, eventually getting to a point where that was all I saw, nothing but warm, bright white light. I stayed in that moment for a little while, nothing being said, nothing being shown to me, just immersed in the light and it felt amazing. After my time was finished in the feeling of the light, my body quickly began travelling back through space, not towards the earth but to a point where the whole of space got smaller and smaller, to where I saw nothing but black. Suddenly, I popped out of my own eye and saw myself standing in the field I used to go to and meditate in. After that meditation I ran all throughout the house trying to explain what happened, but nobody understood. Through my daily practices of meditation and yoga, through the books I was reading and getting into tarot, I would end up being called to leave that life behind for a greater purpose. During a deep meditation one day and pulling tarot cards I was told that I needed to leave Pennsylvania, I needed to leave my family behind, I needed to leave my children, my wife and the life that I had come to know for years behind. I was told that I needed to pack my things up in my Jeep and move away and that this wasn't just for me, this was for everyone, this was for my wife, for my children and all the family members who had come to rely on me and my presence. This was for the lives of the people I would come to touch along the way, the friendships I would make, for the impact that I was going to have on the world. Regardless of how it was going to look to everyone else I was at a different stage in my journey and I needed to honor what GOD had in store for me. After all the things I saw in meditation I no longer felt the power to argue or deny what was being shown to me, I had a clear understanding, I finally became a believer, wholeheartedly.

Moving to Tennessee was and still is an amazing experience in my growth. The synchronicities that have taken place from the time I first arrived to even as I write this book feels like infinite intelligence is guiding me to my higher purpose. The people I have met here, the resources of information that have been put in front of my face paired with the habits I have learned and put into practice have expanded my view of the role I play on this planet in a huge way. From my daily thankfulness journal, to what I call my "power mornings", I have fostered an internal intention and bond with myself that cannot be broken. I have finally found a peace within myself that I accept. I no longer feel the need to be searching for acceptance from others, I no longer feel the need to take things out on myself, nor do I feel the desire to associate in that realm of low vibrational thinking any longer. As some would say, I have seen the light, I have come to trust in love and accept that GOD is always in control and has always been, I just didn't see it at the time. I have come to believe in having a positive impact on the lives of others around the world, I believe that it is my purpose in life to help others with their struggles by sharing mine, by using my knowledge, experiences and creative abilities to develop pathways for others to gain access to the same enlightenment I have gained. I've come to believe that it is all our purpose in life to love ourselves first, for my belief in oneness states that a true love for one, is a true love for all. Although I had to struggle throughout my life to come to this realization, I am filled with the overwhelming sense that this wasn't about me, as my ego would've previously had me believe, no, these struggles were for us all. As I sit here today, in Murfreesboro, TN at 42yrs old sharing with you my personal experiences, my only hope is that through them no one is left to feel alone, nobody is left to feel that life serves no purpose and is just a meaningless existence, that no one is left to feel that the burden they carry is too much to bear. I truly assure you my friends that this is far from the truth, and as the beautiful saying goes "the truth shall set you free."

Spigelmeyer jr

ABOUT THE AUTHOR

This is the first book by Timothy Spigelmeyer jr but his passion for helping others comes from his spiritual awakening as much as from his past experiences. He genuinely believes that nobody should ever feel alone, no one should ever be made to feel like they don't matter in life and that everyone deserves a chance to live a life full of love, abundance and prosperity

Made in the USA
Columbia, SC
28 May 2021